KIRBY

Published by Tate Publishing & Enterprises, LLC
127 E. Trade Center Terrace | Mustang, Oklahoma 73064 USA
1.888.361.9473 | www.tatepublishing.com

Tate Publishing is committed to excellence in the publishing industry. The company reflects the philosophy established by the founders, based on Psalm 68:11,

"The Lord gave the word and great was the company of those who published it."

Book design copyright © 2008 by Tate Publishing, LLC. All rights reserved.
Editing by Kylie Lyons
Cover and Interior design by Kandi Evans

Published in the United States of America

ISBN: 978-1-60696-317-3
1. Biography & Autobiography: Sports: Baseball/Military
10.10.23

J. Terry Johnson

KIRBY

From the BASEBALL Field to the BATTLEFIELD

O CAPTAIN! MY CAPTAIN

BY WALT WHITMAN

O Captain my Captain! our fearful trip is done,
The ship has weathered every rack, the prize we sought is won,
The port is near, the bells I hear, the people all exulting,
While follow eyes the steady keel, the vessel grim and daring;
But O heart! heart! heart!
O the bleeding drops of red,
Where on the deck my Captain lies,
Fallen cold and dead.

O Captain! my Captain! rise up and hear the bells;
Rise up—for you the flag is flung for you the bugle trills,
For you bouquets and ribboned wreaths for you the shores
a-crowding,
For you they call, the swaying mass, their eager faces turning;
Here Captain! dear father!
This arm beneath your head!
It is some dream that on the deck,
You've fallen cold and dead.

My Captain does not answer, his lips are pale and still;
My father does not feel my arm, he has no pulse nor will;
The ship is anchored safe and sound, its voyage closed and done;
From fearful trip the victor ship comes in with object won;
Exult O shores, and ring O bells!
But I, with mournful tread,
Walk the deck my Captain lies,
Fallen cold and dead.

DEDICATION

This book is dedicated to those who coach young men and women to be responsible adults. Men like Dick Birmingham and Charlie Wilcox contribute more to our society than many who enjoy a higher profile in the halls of Congress or on the screen sets of Hollywood. I salute them, along with teachers, parents, ministers and other adults who invest themselves in the lives of our teenagers.

ACKNOWLEDGMENTS

The story of Kirby's life has been in my heart for many years. Each Memorial Day reminds me of the ultimate sacrifice Kirby made for his country and for the dream that all nations of the world might one day live in freedom. I pay homage to all who have worn the uniform on behalf of such a noble cause.

Many have offered anecdotes about Kirby and his adolescent years. I am indebted to Bill Lemery, Doug Mitchell, Dick Birmingham, Charles and Bettye Wilcox, and Linda Lindsay for their recollections of those eventful years in the late fifties and early sixties. Some of the incidents and conversations I have added are imaginary, but the core of the book is based upon actual events.

I am grateful for the newspaper accounts that appeared in the sports section of the *Springfield Leader and Press* in 1959. Many of these articles were written by Marty Eddlemon, who was a genuine friend of the

American Legion baseball program. These articles comprise the framework for chapters nine, ten, and eleven.

The crew at Tate Publishing provided me with invaluable assistance in editing, layout, graphic design, and printing of the book. A special tip of the hat to Richard Tate, Kylie Lyons, and Kandi Evans, who lent their professional skills to the project's completion.

Finally, I salute John Ashcroft, a former classmate, who has distinguished himself in many roles of public service. Now heading his own consulting firm in Washington, D.C., John has been elected governor and United States senator by the citizens of Missouri, and in 2001 was named United States attorney general by President George W. Bush. He graciously consented to write the foreword to *Kirby* as his own expression of appreciation and admiration of a dear friend.

CONTENTS

FOREWORD

*O*n those occasions when I need to escape the pressures imposed by a busy work schedule, I allow my mind to reconnect with the pastoral scenes of the Missouri Ozarks. The roll of the land, the sound of the rivers and streams all remind me of the quieter, gentler days of my boyhood. My trips home are always refreshing experiences.

That's not to say that everything was idyllic in my childhood. Like any family, the Ashcrofts had their share of tough times. But in the fifties, Springfield, Missouri, was a great place for boys to grow into young men.

Although I played football and basketball as a kid, some of my fondest memories were from the baseball diamond. Truthfully, we rarely had a diamond. More often, we played "rounders" in a park, or three-man teams in a field, or whiffle ball in a friend's backyard. We were "die-hard" St. Louis Cardinals fans and dreamed of the day when we would drive the ball onto the Pavilion roof "a la Musial" in St. Louis's old Busch Stadium on Grand Avenue.

My earliest memory of being "coached" in a team sport was while playing baseball with some classmates from Hickory Hills School. Our coach, Charlie Wilcox, was a jocular, energetic parent who shaped a small band of twelve- and thirteen-year-old kids into a respectable little league baseball team. Charlie was the epitome of a father who lived out his athletic dreams through the accomplishments of his highly talented son, Kirby. I came to count both as dear friends.

One day, after squeaking out a narrow victory over a menacing rival, Charlie took our entire team to a local root beer stand. In those days, a frosty mug of root beer cost a nickel. Instead of ordering a single mug for each of the team members, Charlie instructed the store operator, "Fill 'em up!" I didn't get to drink much soda at my house. For me to remember that incident, fifty years later, lets you know what a big deal it was for me and for most of my thirsty teammates. We drank our fair share of root beer—and then some.

I spent two years at Parkview High School with Kirby and the gang from Hickory Hills before our family moved back to the north side of town. Kirby and I kept in touch, but we developed new friends and new interests. He became a popular leader at Parkview, while I was part of the "crew" jumpstarting the newest public school in town, Hillcrest High School.

On the football field, the Hillcrest Hornets were no match for the mighty Vikings from Parkview High. Led by their captain, Larry Westmoreland, the Vikings won the Ozark Conference Championship my senior year. Kirby played on that talented squad. I quarterbacked the Hornets and, on a couple of busted plays, happened to score two touchdowns against Parkview. But at the end of the game, the valiant Vikings were the "conquering heroes," and the Hillcrest Hornets were just another notch on their belts.

Vietnam was a most challenging chapter in the history of our nation. On one hand, the United States was keeping its commitments to defend its allies in harmony with pre-existing international treaties and pacts. On the other hand, more than fifty thousand Americans lost their lives halfway around the world. Kirby Wilcox was among the thousands of brave men and women who answered the call to defend the cause of freedom. Having graduated from West Point, he would not have had it any other way.

I salute my friend and former classmate Terry Johnson for capturing the innocence of teenagers who grew up on the sandlots of Mid-America in the 1950s. *Kirby* is a tribute to men like mentor-coaches Charlie Wilcox and Dick Birmingham, who invested much of their adult lives in developing our nation's youth. We applaud their priorities and pray that there will always be those who make such sacrifices to encourage the idealism and dreams of young men and women.

And I cannot help but tip my hat to all of America's young warriors, present and past, who put their careers on hold to serve our nation in a time of war. Kirby Wilcox, and those of his character, must never be forgotten.

John Ashcroft
U.S. Attorney General, 2001–2005

THE BOYS FROM HICKORY HILLS

The outfield grass was scraggly and parched, having turned a light shade of brown more than a month ago. The infield, being hard as a billiard table, turned routine ground balls into an adventure. The long summer days had taken their toll on West Nichols Park, but the Kiwanis league playoffs were underway, and the games had to be played regardless of the field's fatigued condition.

We had drawn the Lions for our first game in the tournament. Sponsored by the Ideal Tire Company, the Ideal Boys (a mistaken moniker if there ever was one) had limped into the playoffs. Unless we played better baseball than we did the last time our two teams met, the "Boys" wouldn't make it to the second round.

It wasn't that the Lions were a better team—we had split two games with them during the regular season—

but they were more unpredictable than other teams in our league. On any given day, they could bury you in the first three innings.

The Lions excelled in two areas: They were as fast as jackrabbits and as cocky as Banty roosters left in charge of the barnyard. Starting for the Lions were three black players, the only African-Americans in the entire league. Most of their other players attended the fashionable Hickory Hills School near Springfield's best-known country club of the same name. From where we sat, there was a "snob factor" at work whenever we played the boys from Hickory Hills.

One of the black players, Ray Looney, was the ace pitcher for the Lions. He was a southpaw who mixed a hard fastball with a sweeping curve. It was rare for us to see a left-handed pitcher, and no one our age threw a curveball that hooked as much as Looney's. His only weakness was his frequent lapse of control. The rap on the street was that if you could get a few runs off Looney in the early innings, he would collapse like a accordian-folder.

Today, Looney had his good "stuff." We had managed one run off him in the first three innings, and it had been unearned. Fortunately, our best pitcher, Bud Smith, had held the Lions scoreless during those three frames. If the Lions were to advance in the playoffs, they would need to find a way to solve Bud's fastball and his pinpoint control.

Charlie Wilcox was the affable coach for the Lions. He was a gabby sort of fellow who could strike up a conversation with the foul pole. From his third-base coaching box, Wilcox would flash signs to his hitters and keep them focused on the game with his constant banter. When not on the field, you could usually find him smoking a cigar beneath the bleachers.

In center field for the Lions was the coach's son, Kirby Wilcox. There was an air about Kirby that was unsettling to me. He was chatty like his dad but a little condescending in his remarks to players on the opposing team. I especially disliked the way he and his dad directed negative comments to my teammates and me when we were at the plate.

"Come on, Ray!," Mr. Wilcox would yell to his pitcher. "This guy can't swing the bat fast enough to hit your high hard one! Sit him down on the bench where he belongs."

In our division, two umpires worked the games, one behind the plate and the other covering all three bases. Junior Kinser, a star basketball player for the Central High School Bulldogs, was the infield umpire that night. He had been assigned to call some of our games earlier in the summer and always handled the task professionally.

Between innings he would make small talk with those of us who played the infield. I liked him as an umpire and stood slightly in awe of his celebrity status at the local high school.

Kirby Wilcox led off the top of the fourth inning with a flare to right field that fell between the outstretched gloves of the right fielder and me. It was one of those "cheap hits" that results more from luck than talent. As the saying goes, "All base hits look like line drives in the box score the next morning." But there Kirby stood on first base, smiling and enjoying the cheers from the Lions' bench. I was disgusted at myself for not being able to reach the ball, and now I had to watch him preen and smirk as if he had won the game with a "walk-off homerun."

"Atta boy!" yelled Mr. Wilcox from his third-base coaching box. "Stay alert," he continued as he began to flash signs to both Kirby and the next batter who was about to assume his place at the plate.

Our entire team was aware that Kirby had better than average speed and, if given an opportunity, was a threat to steal second base. He took a healthy lead off first base, diving back to the bag when Bud Smith tried to pick him off. This was where the Lions were exceptionally tough. They created pressure on the base paths, often causing the defense to make costly errors.

As Bud looked into the plate for a sign from our catcher, Mike Cunningham, I signaled to our shortstop that I would cover second base in the event that Kirby tried to steal. Bud threw a pitchout, and, sure enough, Kirby broke for second base. The race between ball and runner was on.

Mike's throw to second was slightly high, but it beat Kirby to the bag. I straddled the base, snagged the ball out of the air, and applied the tag just as he arrived in an enormous cloud of dust.

"Safe!" Kinser shouted, spreading his arms out flat.

"No way!" I protested. "He slid right into my glove. How can you call him safe?"

"You missed him," Kinser replied as he walked away from second base.

Kirby got up, dusting himself off, smiling like a possum. I was pretty sure he knew that he had been tagged out, but I wasn't sure what to do about Kinser.

"How could you miss that call?" I yelled at the umpire, my voice raised in anger.

"That's enough," Kinser retorted, shooting me a look that affirmed his authority in the situation.

Looking back, it must have been that my pride was wounded. Mike's throw to second base was in plenty of time for me to apply the tag, sending Kirby back to the bench as out number one. Someone was to blame for his

21

not being called out, and I didn't want it to be me. So I took the issue to Kinser one more time.

"You need glasses?" I asked. It was futile to press the argument, but I just couldn't let it drop. Kirby had gotten away with a steal that he didn't deserve and was acting entirely too smug about the whole matter.

Kinser called time out, signaling to the home plate umpire to suspend play. And then he walked over to me and looked me squarely in the eyes.

"Young man, I called the play the way I saw it," Kinser began. "The runner was safe. If you have another word to say about the call, you can watch the rest of the game from the bleachers. Do I make myself clear?"

I made no verbal response. There was nothing more to be said. So I tugged at the bill of my cap, kicked some dirt with my cleats, and reassumed my position at second base.

The Lions went on to defeat the Ideal Boys that night, but that's not what I remember most about the game. Competitive sports teach us how to win, how to lose, and how to deal with some of the more important issues in life. I learned my lesson about arguing with umpires. Kinser put me in my place and left me with a healthy scar from our encounter on the field.

But the lesson that stayed with me the longest had to do more with judging people without really knowing them. I didn't like Kirby Wilcox. To me, he was arrogant, haughty, and not the kind of person I would ever consider having as a friend. If I never saw him again, it would be all right with me. Little did I know how much our lives would become enmeshed over the next four years.

Jarrett Junior High
Springfield, Missouri

ROCK 'N' ROLL

*M*y two years at Jarrett Junior High School were prologue to four of the best years a teenage boy could ever imagine. Released from the protective cocoon of elementary school, I found junior high to be a much tougher environment, both inside and outside the classroom. The course work was more demanding, social life became more interesting, and extracurricular activities were far more challenging than anything I had experienced before.

My dad had attended Jarrett a generation before I arrived on the scene, and some of his teachers were still in the classroom. The three-story building was dark and foreboding. Ceilings were high, hallways were dimly lit, and a throng of bodies pushed its way through the corridors hourly between class sessions.

Each day, fights erupted on the dirt and graveled playground, resulting in students being suspended or disciplined in other ways. I worked hard to keep my distance from the roughnecks that enjoyed picking fights whenever school let out.

Grades came easy for me; making the school's basketball team did not. Needing to cut the squad from twelve players to ten, Coach Herb Weston called me aside after practice one afternoon and said, "I wish I could keep you on the team, son, but this is the end of the road for you." The news wasn't a surprise. Even I could tell basketball was not my competitive sport.

So I spent the rest of the year participating in the intramural football, basketball, and softball programs. We were the proud Mustangs of Homeroom 114. Although the games were fun, none of it compared to being on the baseball diamond in the heat of the summer. I lived for baseball.

Knowing that I might need a little help with social life, Mom enrolled me in a dance class that was offered each week at the downtown YWCA. Bettye Vogel, a courageous soul whose son, Charlie, was in the class, was our teacher. Working with junior high school students, she had to be a "woman for all seasons"—instructor, disciplinarian, counselor, and chaperone. Most evenings could be described as "organized chaos," while on a few occasions it approached "bedlam." But we did learn to dance.

There was a good mix of boys and girls in the dance class, and most of them attended Jarrett. A few were in the square dance troupe we had had at Sunshine Elementary, but Mrs. Vogel let us know from the very first class that what she would be teaching was considerably more advanced than "do-si-do." Over the course of several weeks, we were taught how to waltz, do the cha-cha, and even a few tango steps. For those of us with two left feet, we never got very far with the tango.

What we all wanted Mrs. Vogel to teach us was how to "jitterbug" to the early sounds of "rock 'n' roll." Bill Haley and The Comets had just come out with their classic, "Rock Around the Clock," and Chuck Berry was on the charts with "Maybellene." Elvis would not make his breakthrough until the next year, but the stage was set for a revolution in music. We were all eager to get in step with the new beat that was being played over KICK 1340 AM, the top-forty radio station in Springfield.

"All right, class," Mrs. Vogel would begin, "pair up, boy-girl, boy-girl." That was the hardest part of the class for me—asking a girl to be my dance partner.

Then Mrs. Vogel would turn the record player on and begin the drill. "Toe, heel. Toe, heel. Back step," she repeated over and over, checking each pair to see that they were getting the basic step. "Toe, heel. Toe, heel. Back step." Once the rudimentary steps were in place, we began to learn spins and turns and other variations that made the dance much more interesting.

In addition to the dance instruction, Mrs. Vogel spent part of the class time teaching us good manners, courtesy, and a few tips on "boy-girl" relationships. It wasn't a "cotillion" class *per se,* but it was along that order. She honed our social skills and prepared us for the dating scene that lay just around the corner.

On the last night of the dance class, Mrs. Vogel gave each boy and girl a card that was numbered one to ten. Before any record was played that night, the boys had to ask the girls to reserve a certain dance for them. With one exception, each dance had to be with a different partner. The exception was that you could ask one girl to fill two spots on your card.

I didn't have to think long whom I wanted to ask for dances one and ten. Frankie Whipple was "Miss Personality" and seemed to show some interest in me. There she was across the room, wearing a pink poodle skirt and white bobby socks. What did I have to lose?

"Frankie," I managed to say softly, "would you reserve dances one and ten for me?" She fluttered her eyes, smiled like sunshine, and said, "I will. Thank you." And with that nervous approach, I took a giant step forward in my social awareness.

Three weeks later, Mrs. Vogel hosted a large dance

at the Doling Pavilion in North Springfield. She invited our dance class and students from another class she had taught to join in the fun. It was the first time I had ever really gone to a dance, but, fortified by the lessons, I was ready to give it a try. Frankie was there. That made it even more appealing.

And someone else was there. Over in a corner of the darkened room was Kirby Wilcox, accompanied by a few of his friends from Hickory Hills. He was the center of attention, loud and laughing at his own wisecracks. If we happened to bump into each other, I would speak, but I had no intention of going out of my way to say hello.

As the evening progressed, I found myself dancing almost every tune with Frankie. She was easy to talk to and kept me from feeling self-conscious about my clumsy feet. She had tossed her penny loafers off to the side of the room long ago and was dancing in her bobby socks. Everything was very comfortable, and then I felt a tap on my shoulder.

"Mind if I cut in?" It was Kirby, standing there as if I owed him some debt and he was ready to collect his payment.

"I guess not," I managed to say, knowing inside that was certainly not how I felt about the matter.

Kirby and Frankie danced into the middle of the crowded floor to the dreamy music of the Penguins, singing their top-forty hit, "Earth Angel." I was left standing there, a bit hurt, considerably embarrassed, and hot as a jalapeño pepper. This bloke from the country club side of the tracks had messed up what had been a perfect evening. Where did he get such nerve?

The remaining days at Jarrett sped by quickly. I spent only two years there, seventh and eighth grades. Until our class came along, junior high school was a three-year program, extending through the ninth grade. But a new public high school was under construction just two blocks from my house, and the Springfield School Board had decided to make the high school curriculum designed for grades nine through twelve beginning in the fall of 1956. Our class would be the first true high school "freshmen" Springfield had had in many years.

OPENING THE DOORS AT PARKVIEW

*a*s we anticipated the opening bell on the first day of classes, those of us who were freshmen at the brand new high school were as energized as a row of thoroughbreds awaiting the starter's call at the Kentucky Derby. And why shouldn't we have been excited? This was what we had been talking about all summer. We were the inaugural freshman class at Parkview High School.

The physical complex for the new high school was an architectural marvel. It looked nothing like those other school buildings in town. None of that red brick and classical styling that belonged to the past generation. This structure had been designed for a new age in education.

Parkview was situated on an elevated plateau, overlooking Fassnight Park and the creek that meandered through it. The building's design featured split-level classroom wings, elbowed in the middle and extending like huge arms toward Campbell Street. Walls made almost entirely of glass let in abundant light to make the corridors bright and cheery. This new school was, quite literally, the talk of the town.

On the first day of classes, students had gathered in the spacious lobby adjacent to the offices and school library. They were visiting with old friends, who introduced them to new friends who became their best friends within the first week. I was chatting with Dan Lowry, a lifelong pal and also a member of the freshman class. In our pre-school years, we had grown up almost like brothers and had actually lived together while our dads were serving in the military during World War II.

"Where's your first class?" I asked.

"I have Mr. Sheeley first hour," Dan replied. "How about you?"

"Coach Weston for civics class," I said. Mr. Weston had made the move from Jarrett to coach the men's basketball program at Parkview High. "We all know he's a good basketball coach," I continued, "but I wonder what on earth he knows about civics."

Noticing some commotion coming from a corner of the crowded lobby, I asked, "Are those kids over there from Hickory Hills?"

"Yeah, I'm pretty sure they are," Dan replied. "I recognize a few of them."

"Why don't they attend high school at Hickory Hills?" I asked.

"Their school only goes through the eighth grade," Dan said. He lived closer to that area of town and knew more of the Hickory Hills students.

Then I saw Kirby in the crowd. He was laughing, talking loud, putting on a show for some of the freshmen girls who had drawn close to him like flies buzzing around a jar of molasses.

He was dressed modestly in blue jeans that were rolled up at the bottom, showing his white socks and black loafers. His shirt was a button-down Madras plaid. Some of the other guys, who were a little more fashion conscious, wore casual black slacks with a little buckle in the back and pink shirts. The "ivy league" look was the fashion rage, and black with pink were the hot colors for those who cared about those things.

"Do you know Kirby Wilcox?" I asked Dan.

"Not very well," he answered. "I know who he is, but we don't run much in the same circles. I heard he plans to go out for the freshman football team." And then Dan asked, "Are you planning to try out for football?"

"I'm not sure," I answered honestly. "The first meeting is Wednesday, and I've been thinking about it but haven't made up my mind." I knew for sure that I wanted to get involved in student government right away and play baseball in the spring, but football was still a *maybe*.

The bell suddenly rang, signaling that classes would begin in ten minutes. I said good-bye to Dan and headed for Coach Weston's civics class. The halls were jammed with students streaming like mice through a maze until each found his or her respective first-hour classroom. It was time for the new school year's scholastic exercises to begin.

Coach Weston was a tall, well-groomed man who maintained a stern expression on his face while lecturing the class. Dressed in a salt-and-pepper tweed suit and an expensive silk tie, he kept his suit jacket on throughout the entire class period. He enjoyed a reputation for being a "no-nonsense" kind of coach, and that discipline accompanied him into the classroom.

"You may address me as Mr. Weston," he said as part of his opening comments. "The basketball team calls me Coach Weston, but this civics class is not the basketball team." I made a note on my fresh sheet of notebook paper, "*Mister* Weston."

As Mr. Weston began to outline the content of his first day's lesson plan, he posed a few simple questions to the class.

"What form of government do we have in the United

States?" he asked. It was a "sucker" question, and a red-headed boy on the front row took the bait.

"A democracy," the eager student offered, confident in his own ignorance.

"Well, not exactly," Mr. Weston replied.

Another hand shot up on the back row, and I recognized that it was Kirby when I heard his voice. He said, "Sir, we have a constitutional republic."

Mr. Weston complimented Kirby for his correct answer and then asked him his name. "Kirby Wilcox, sir," he answered without hesitation.

Chalk one up for the boy from Hickory Hills, I thought to myself. *Before the day is over, he will be on his way to becoming the teacher's pet.*

When the bell rang, I headed for my second-hour class—English I with Mrs. Ferne Westbrooke. She was another teacher who had made the move from Jarrett to Parkview. To my relief, Kirby wasn't in that class, and I didn't see him the rest of the day.

Kirby
Freshman at Parkview High

FRESHMAN FOOTBALL

*a*fter weighing my options, I had decided to attend the organizational meeting for those who wanted to play on the freshman football team. The varsity and junior varsity squads had already been engaged in "two-a-day" practices during the August heat, but now it was time to organize a freshman team. Several friends from Jarrett were planning to play, so I decided to join them.

Head Coach Orville Pottenger introduced his staff and explained how important it was for a new school to establish a winning tradition in its athletic program.

"You freshmen will have an opportunity to do something no one else has done," Coach Pottenger began. "You will be the first class to play football all four years at Parkview High School. By the time you are seniors," he continued, "I predict you will be Ozark Conference champions."

Some of the assistant coaches chimed in with comments regarding their expectations for the team. After that, they were ready to get underway.

Once those of us who were trying out for the team had signed some paperwork, we were issued practice gear, assigned a locker, and told to report the next afternoon for our first workout session. A technician fitted us for rubber-molded mouthpieces to keep our teeth from getting busted out. I looked at the helmet in my hand and wondered what I was stepping into.

The next afternoon, fifty or more boys reported to the practice field for time trials and team conditioning. We were put through a lengthy set of calisthenics and ordered to run laps around the field until we almost dropped.

"Get the lead out, Westmoreland!" Assistant Coach Bob Lechner yelled. Larry Westmoreland was probably the best football talent among the freshmen. He was a large-framed kid who wanted to play center. From all reports, he had a "lock" on the position and would likely be a starter for the junior varsity squad as well. His size and popularity made him an easy target for the coaches' barbs.

It was a tough first day. Several prospects checked in their equipment before the session was over. Those of us who continued ached in a few places where we never knew our bodies had muscles. Mercifully, a whistle blew and we were sent to the showers. Our first practice was over.

The boys locker room after football practice was a bizarre scene. Most of us had gotten over the embarrassment of undressing in front of the guys, because we had done that in junior high school physical education classes. But the horseplay that accompanied these young stallions as they showered and dressed resembled a fraternity's initiation party. At any moment, there would be buck-naked boys "flipping" each other with their wet towels, as if they were gladiators in the Roman Coliseum. And the upperclassmen reserved their best taunts for us lowly freshmen.

"Listen up, freshmen!" junior quarterback Ed Stracke yelled with noticeable authority in his voice. The room came to an unsettled hush. "Next Monday, when you come to practice, there had better not be any of you ninth-graders with long hair. If your hair is not cut in a flattop by then, the upperclassmen will cut it for you."

I wondered how Coach Pottenger had forgotten to include that item in his opening remarks. No mention of "hair" or "haircuts" in the coaches' remarks. I had never worn a flattop but determined right then that I was due for a new "'do."

After the first two weeks of practice, Coach Lechner had decided that Kirby would be the freshman first-string fullback. I was assigned to be his backup. That meant he and I were going to be bumping into each other quite often on the football field. The first-string backfield would run a series of plays, and then the second team would do the same. We learned draws and dives and slants and sweeps; nothing fancy, just the ABC's of high school football.

Because Kirby had a gift for gab and his own way of schmoozing the coaches, he was well-known and easily liked by our mentors on the field. But he too was a target of their stinging criticisms.

"Get your head up, Wilcox, not your rear!" Coach Lechner would yell. "And the play runs left of tackle, not right!"

"Wilcox, quit tip-toeing through the line," Lechner would add. "If you can't hit the hole with more force than that, I'm going to see if one of the cheerleaders can show you how to do it."

Kirby would do what we all did when we got chewed out—he picked himself up, got back in formation, and tried it all over again. The process, however, began to bond the team together, as we felt some empathy for one another when the reprimands got a little rough and personal. More than once I found myself saying to Kirby, "Let it go. Coach must be having a bad day."

The freshmen played only two games that year. Both

were against the freshman team from our crosstown rival—the Central High School Bullpups. In the locker room, prior to the first game, we all got to experience the uneasy sensation of having "butterflies" fluttering in our stomachs. Before they could settle, it was time for the opening kickoff.

Kirby wore high-top cleats, white football pants, and a green jersey with the number "30" stitched in yellow satin across the front and back. During the first half, he ran several offensive series at the fullback slot. I started at right cornerback for the defense.

The game was scoreless, with neither offensive unit able to sustain a drive. Suddenly, from the sideline, I heard the referee's whistle blow, signaling time-out on the field.

"Someone's injured!" I overheard Jerry Adams, our nose tackle, shout.

"Who's down?" I asked.

"I think it's Wilcox," Adams said hesitantly. "Can't be sure."

The coaches were out on the field attending to the downed player. Once they had him on his feet, I could tell it was Kirby. He was limping as he came toward the sidelines and was experiencing considerable pain. Then I heard Coach Lechner yell my name. I pulled on my helmet and sprinted toward him.

"Get in there at fullback," Lechner ordered.

Not waiting for further instructions, I dashed onto the field and took my place in the huddle.

"What's up with Wilcox?" asked Dick Davis, one of our two halfbacks in a traditional "T-formation" offense.

"Not sure, but I think he twisted a knee," I managed to answer between gasps for air. For a moment, I thought I was going to hyperventilate.

From our own thirty-five-yard line, we ran a sweep of right end with Davis carrying the ball. He gained fourteen yards and a first down. That seemed easy enough.

Maybe we should try that play again, I thought to myself as I returned to the huddle.

I listened carefully to the next play being called, wanting to make sure that I knew the count for the snap of the ball. To my surprise, the play was a fullback draw between the center and the right guard. They had called "my number."

"On two. Break!" the quarterback said. We all took our positions and got in a three-point stance.

"Hut one. Hut two." Westmoreland had snapped the football.

I turned my body to the right, faking a run in that direction, then bolted forward toward the hole that was opened by the offensive line. Feeling the ball tucked into my stomach, I broke through the line with all of the speed my football cleats would allow.

No one could have predicted what happened next. It was as if all of the defensive players were moving in slow-motion. Perhaps expecting another sweep around our right end, the defense had shifted to that side of the field. I broke through the line, veered hard to the left, and then headed for the goal line. Nothing but open field was in front of me. By the time I stumbled into the end zone, I had covered fifty-one yards and scored our first touchdown.

From that day until the end of my sophomore year, I ran offensive plays with the first team. Kirby seemed to accept my good fortune well enough. In fact, the turn of events drew us a little closer together. I began to lay down some of the prejudices I had held about the boy from Hickory Hills. It was the breakthrough we needed to begin building a genuine friendship.

Kirby
Summer 1957

VALIANT VIKINGS

*a*lthough drawn together through athletics, Kirby and I ran in different social circles our first two years at Parkview. Most of my friends had come from Jarrett or were in student government; his friends had come from Hickory Hills. Many of his closest friends were on the football or baseball team. I participated in music and drama; he had little use for either. With the exception of Mr. Weston's civics course, we were not in any classes together.

Yet, I came to like Kirby more than I ever thought possible as I began to see what lay beneath his boisterous, "in-your-face" veneer. Kirby hid his own shyness and insecurities behind a "macho" mask. He struggled, as we all did at times, with finding himself and not simply living out someone else's dream.

Kirby spent his spare time working at the Conoco service station that was owned and operated by his dad.

Charlie Wilcox adored his son and believed Kirby could be "number one" in just about anything he aspired to do. It was not uncommon, however, for Mr. Wilcox to offer his son an earful of advice, whether solicited or not.

On several occasions, I listened to Kirby lament that he couldn't be everything his dad wanted him to be. He wasn't number one on the football team; he wasn't president of his class; his grades were good, but not all A's. Mr. Wilcox's attempts to help his son were often interpreted by Kirby as being intrusive.

I proposed my simplistic solution to his frustration. "Why don't you just tell him to back off?"

"It's not that easy," Kirby answered. "My dad's been good to me. I don't want to let him down. I just need him to give me a little space to do my own thing."

"Can you quit your job so that you don't have to be around him all the time?" I said, playing the "wise fool" we sophomores had become.

"I'll work it out," Kirby said dismissively, and I knew it was time to drop the subject. But his struggles in these areas revealed a vulnerable side to a friend who appeared, on the surface, to have his life all put together.

—

The home phone rang late one night. Studying for an exam, I picked it up quickly before it disturbed my parents, who had already retired for the evening.

"Hello."

It was Doug Mitchell, a long-time baseball chum who also happened to be the best dancer in Mrs. Vogel's dance class. Doug had a great baseball card collection, but he also had an outstanding set of 45-rpm records, including all the latest hits being played by KICK. He had found a junky little store selling used records. These were recent hit singles that were being discarded by juke-box owners once the tunes had lost their popularity.

"Sorry to be calling so late. Have you got a minute?" Doug asked.

"Sure. What's up?" I replied.

"What would you think about getting together with Dick Davis and Jim O'Bryant to form a quartet?" Doug inquired. "We might be able to perform at the class talent show."

That was a novel thought. I loved to sing, but the idea of being part of a singing group was not on my radar screen.

"Who would we get to play backup for us?" I asked, unsure of whether we could ever pull it off. "I don't want to do any 'barbershop quartet' numbers or anything like that."

Doug agreed. "Charlie McCord said he would accompany us," he responded. "He plays the piano by ear. But we could also use a drummer. Do you know anyone who's good with the drums?"

"How about Dan Lowry?" I offered. "He plays drums."

"Great," Doug said. "Let's see if we can get everyone together after classes tomorrow and set up a time to practice."

Charles McCord invited the group to practice at his house the following Saturday. Doug brought a few of his records, and we gave them a spin. In just a matter of minutes, Charles picked out the tunes on the piano, Dan found a comfortable beat, and the rest of us were belting out the familiar lyrics of "Silhouettes" and "At the Hop."

And with that, "The Four Flames and Two Flickers" were born. What we lacked in talent, we made up for in showmanship, dressed in our white sport coats, red bow ties, and flaming red carnations. The group only stayed together for a year, singing at the class talent assembly and a few school-sponsored banquets.

One day, I encountered Kirby in the lunchroom. "What did you think about the talent assembly?" I asked him, fishing for a compliment.

"It was all right," he answered.

"And the Four Flames and Two Flickers?" I probed, leaving myself open to his candid appraisal.

"You want the truth?" he said. I knew this wasn't going to be what I wanted to hear.

"Sure," I replied with resignation.

"The name's clever, but you guys could use some more practice," he said with a big smile on his face. "And tell Davis to sing on key or stick with playing football."

I gave up on football after our sophomore season. My sport was baseball, and even though I had enjoyed some success on the junior varsity gridiron team, I had no long-term interest in the game. Kirby excelled at baseball, but he decided to stay with football as his fall sport. He could compete in baseball during the spring and summer. He gave me a hard time over my decision to "check it in."

"What were you thinking?" Kirby chortled when he heard I had told Coach Pottenger to write me off the football team roster. "I thought you were tougher than that."

"Football is a waste of my time," I replied. "You know how much I love baseball, but it's not the same with football. I have no passion for the sport. Besides, I need that time for homework and student government."

After serving my freshman year as class president, I had been on the Student Council Cabinet my sophomore year and was elected to serve as Election Commissioner my junior year. One of my teachers had noted on my report card that I had missed her class an equivalent of one-fourth of the year. Almost all of those absences were due either to student government activities or my playing on the school's baseball team.

Just as our dissimilar high school interests took us in different directions, it was baseball that always pulled Kirby and me back together. We played junior varsity baseball our freshman year at Parkview, and both of us made the varsity as sophomores. It was a new coach for the summer American Legion Junior baseball team, however, who became the catalyst for Kirby and me becoming the very best of friends.

BIRMINGHAM'S BOYS

*a*merican Legion Junior baseball was a major summertime event in Springfield. Having lost its professional minor league team years ago, the *Springfield Leader and Press* provided good newspaper coverage for the local teams that competed in the American Legion program. And now that there were two high schools in town, a second Legion team was formed to accommodate the players from Parkview.

Dick Birmingham, a tall, lean, handsome man in his midtwenties, was named the new coach for the Parkview Tastemarks, Legion Post 69. Being an unpaid volunteer, he dedicated himself to the success of the program and sought players who would do the same. As expected, the first year produced few victories, but it did set the stage for better years to come. Having just completed our freshman year, Kirby and I watched superstar Bonus Frost and other upperclassmen from a distance and promised each other that we would become leaders of the squad the next season.

When tryouts were announced the next spring for the 1958 Parkview Legion team, Kirby and I were among the first to show up. Birmingham was still an "unknown quantity" to many of us who aspired to be on the team. He didn't teach or coach at Parkview High. What we did know was that he had played quarterback for the Southwest Missouri State football team, where he had picked up some solid coaching principles. He believed in conditioning, drills, and long hours spent on the practice field.

"Listen up," Birmingham would begin a practice session. "*Prior preparation prevents poor performance.* I want you to remember that. It is the mantra of winners. If you want to win, you must practice—often and with intensity."

Kirby started in left field that year, playing center field when junior Dave Eustis was pitching. I began the year on the bench but won the starting position at second base before the year was over. Although a few juniors with big bats led the team, most of the regular players were from our sophomore class. We were a scruffy-looking crew in old, gray woolen uniforms, with "POST 69" lettered in an arc across the front of our jerseys.

"Coach," Kirby said one afternoon, "are we going to make any overnight trips this year?"

"That all depends," said Birmingham. "It depends on whether we can get some travel funds, and it depends on how well you play in the early part of the season. Show me something, and we'll see what we can do about going on a few trips."

As it happened, we made no trips outside the state of Missouri, playing most of our games at home. When we did travel, it was in car caravans, escorted by an avid, parent-centered fan club. Kirby's parents usually took a car, and he always invited me to join them.

On one occasion, Coach did lease a smelly old Trailways bus for a road trip to Joplin. It wasn't a long trip. In fact, we were home before midnight. But just loading our gear onto a bus instead of the trunks of our parents' cars made us feel like we had made the "big time."

"What are those guys doing in the back of the bus?" I inquired of Bill Lemery, who was seated next to me.

"I think Redfearn and Burtner have got Kirby up to his neck in a poker game," Bill whispered. Before we got home, Kirby had laid down some "lunch money" to the upperclassmen.

The heat that summer was near record levels. Each practice session was more blistering than the one before. Coach Birmingham, dressed each day in white shorts and a white t-shirt, was the consummate hands-on field general. He hit fungoes to the outfield, ground balls to the infield, and pitched batting practice to the entire team. If the heat ever bothered him, he didn't let us know about it.

One day, Coach caught Kirby conducting a gabfest in the outfield instead of shagging flies.

"What's with the convention?" Coach yelled to the outfielders, clustered in center field.

Kirby loved to tease and thought he could get himself and the others off the hook with a wisecrack.

"We were just talking about what a great coach you are and how we want to grow up to be just like you," Kirby quipped with a smirk on his face.

"Wilcox, give me three laps around the field," Birmingham ordered. "And remember, when you're a coach, that's what you do with wiseacres."

After working through a break-even year, it was time for the playoffs. A team had to win two major tournaments in order to have a shot at the state championship game. First came the district tournament, and if successful there, we would have to win the Western Zone tournament, pitting us against some of the best teams from the western half of the state of Missouri. Our first test would be to dethrone our archrival, the Central Pepsi Colas.

"Listen up," Coach said in the same way he began almost every pep talk. "You have come a long way this summer, but this is what it's all about. Just because Central has had the upper hand lately doesn't mean you can't emerge as the champions of this tournament."

Udell McConnell coached the Central Pepsi squad. Being a partial owner in a local sporting goods store, he had found a way to outfit his team with the sharpest-looking uniforms we had seen all year. They used the sleeveless jerseys with short-sleeved undershirts, made popular by the Cincinnati Reds and the Pittsburgh Pirates in the National League. Central looked like the defending Western Zone champions that they were. And they played like it too. We lost our first two games and hung up our spikes for the season.

Although the win-loss record did not reflect it, the summer of 1958 was a pivotal year for the Parkview Legion nine. Brought together from a diverse background, individual players began to function as a team. Where there had been doubt, belief had begun to grow. Coach Birmingham took the collective talent of his raw recruits and forged a brute force, confident of its eventual date with destiny.

Dick Birmingham

THE RED FORD FAIRLANE CONVERTIBLE

*W*hile Kirby was pumping gas at the Conoco station on South Kimbrough, I was coaching three Kiwanis League baseball teams to earn my spending cash. The Mustangs were ten-year-olds and the best in their league. What made them so good was their right-handed pitcher, Steve Rogers, who had a fastball that would have struck out a few players on our American Legion team.

One morning, the Mustangs were in a close ballgame with the Blackhawks, their rivals from the north side of town. Steve was pitching a shutout but was having trouble with his control. After walking two batters, he was more determined than ever to get the ball over the plate. And he did. But this time the Blackhawks' chunky catcher got wood on Steve's fastball, knocking it all the way to the fence for a standup triple. The game was now tied, 2–2, and the go-ahead run was on third base.

I called time and jogged out to the mound to give Steve a little pep talk. To my surprise, tears were trickling down his cheeks. He wasn't used to seeing anyone hit the cover off his fastball.

"Hey, big guy," I said. "No damage done unless this runner on third scores. Just do your thing, and we're going to be all right." Steve struck out the next three batters and hit his own homerun in the bottom half of the inning to win the game.

As the players and I were collecting our gear and congratulating one another for the victory, I saw Kirby walking around the fence and onto the field. He was dressed casually in red Bermuda shorts and a white Izod shirt. I could tell he was excited to tell me some big news.

"What's up?" I asked, surprised to see him at one of my kids' games.

"Come here," he said. "I've got something to show you."

Kirby led me around the fence, behind the bleachers, and into the parking lot. And there it sat…one of the most beautiful cars I could have ever imagined. It was a red and white 1957 Ford Fairlane 500 convertible, with a trendy set of fins highlighting the rear fenders.

"It's mine," he said with a smile spread across his face. "Want me to take you home?"

"You've got to be kidding me," I stammered in total amazement. "Where on earth did this come from?"

"Hop in and I'll tell you," he said.

"Let me see Mrs. Rogers for a minute," I said as I began to sprint back toward the bleachers. "She offered to take me home. Wow! This is unbelievable!"

Having saved some money from working at the service station, and with a little help from his dad, Kirby had acquired the hottest car any sixteen-year-old boy could ever dream of owning. We threw my gear into the trunk and headed for the south side of town. With his left elbow extended out the window and driving with only his right hand on the steering wheel, Kirby looked about as cool as any classmate at Parkview High.

Charlie Wilcox had laid down a few "ground rules" regarding his son's new car. Kirby could have only one other boy in the car at any given time. It was all right to have one boy and two girls, but never more than one boy other than Kirby.

"With only one other boy in the car," Mr. Wilcox had instructed his son, "you will keep your head about you; but with two others, there will be mischief." Kirby was so thrilled to have the car, he might have promised his dad anything, but it was a pledge he was diligent to keep…at least for the first year or so.

Since my sixteenth birthday was still five months

away, and there were no prospects of my having a car of my own, I looked forward to those times when Kirby would offer to pick me up for baseball practice or see if I wanted to go out cruising the popular drive-ins. With its top down, the convertible was worthy of the many double takes we received as we drove all over town.

One day, as we were finishing baseball practice, Kirby said, "Can you get away next week to see the Cardinals play in St. Louis?"

"You mean just the two of us?" I replied. "In your new car?"

"How else do you think we would get there?" he answered with a broad grin across his face. "Dad said I could take one person, and I thought you might like to go with me."

"You're on," I said. "When do we leave and how long do we get to stay?"

The Pittsburgh Pirates were visiting the Cardinals for a five-game series that began with a Sunday double-header in late August. We decided to drive to St. Louis on Monday and catch the last three games. Riding four hours in Kirby's new convertible, top down and breezing along historic U.S. Route 66, was like living a page out of the movies. I had never felt so "grown-up" in all my life.

"Have you decided for sure what you want to do when you graduate from Parkview?" Kirby inquired.

"I'm definitely going to attend SMU," I replied, "but I'm still debating between ministry and law. What about you?"

When Kirby wanted to be serious about a matter, his demeanor changed. The teasing, fun-loving kid suddenly became professorial. It was as if he had morphed into another person, someone ten or twenty years older.

"I'm thinking about applying for West Point," he said, his brow furrowed and his tone deadly serious. "If accepted, I can see myself pursuing a career in the military."

That thought took me by surprise. It was the first time I had ever pictured Kirby in army fatigues. We continued the discussion over the next three days, revealing our innermost feelings about the future. Two boys trying hard to sound like grown men.

The Cardinals lost two of the three games at Busch Stadium. Roberto Clemente, the Pirates All-Star right fielder, put on a hitting clinic with six hits in thirteen at bats. But what Kirby and I came home remembering were the discussions we shared about our faith and our dreams for the future.

Red and White
Ford Fairlane 500 Convertible

PLAYING THE FIELD

*a*lthough preoccupied with playing baseball during the summer, Kirby and I found that dating the Parkview girls made for a little "balance" in our lives. Now that he had a car, and a hot-looking one at that, it was easy to double date for Cokes at the drive-ins, or go to the movies, or attend an occasional dance hosted by one of the social clubs. It was all in good fun; nothing serious, but it added another dimension to our self-awareness of how we stood on the threshold of manhood.

For almost a year, Carol Anderson, a "doe-eyed" brunette, had been wearing my initial ring on a chain around her neck. The official term was "going steady." We met each morning before school began and went out of our way between classes to bump into each other. If someone was having a party, we were inseparable on the dance floor; and whenever we heard Johnny Mathis sing

"The Twelfth of Never," we knew someone had written the lyrics just for us.

Kirby was content to play the field. Even with the car and his natural good looks, he was awkwardly shy at times, needing a push to find the courage to ask someone special for a date. He would rather take a beating than to be turned down by a girl for a Coke date.

"What about getting dates this weekend and going to the movies?" I suggested to Kirby one evening as we were driving home from a Parkview High basketball game. We were midway into our junior year, and the social scene had been a little stale.

"What's on?" he replied.

"I heard 'The Defiant Ones' was really good," I said. "Of course, the girls will probably want to see 'Gigi' or one of those sappy movies."

"I don't know," Kirby said. "You already know who you'll ask, but I always have to start from scratch."

"You could ask Madeline," I proposed. Kirby had dated Madeline Bartling lately. She was a year younger than he, blonde-headed, and rather cute. They made a good-looking couple: he with his athletic build, driving his convertible with its top down, and she with her blonde hair blowing in the wind.

"I guess so," he said without much enthusiasm. "I'll call you and let you know if it works out." Later that evening, I heard from Kirby. Madeline had said yes, and we were on for the Saturday-night movie.

Kirby wheeled by my house in his red and white "limo," this time with its top up and the car spotlessly cleaned, inside and out. He was a stickler for things being neat and in good order. Image was important to Kirby.

In a matter of minutes, Kirby had picked up Madeline, whisked us to Carol's house, and announced that he had a surprise for all of us. He let the top down and steered the red Ford toward the north side of town.

"Where are you going?" I asked when I realized we were not anywhere near the theaters.

"I have a stop to make and someone for you to meet," he replied. "I'm taking you over to the Boys' Club."

Upon arriving at the Boys' Club on north Booneville Street, Kirby hopped out of the car and said, "Stay here for a minute. I'll be right back."

While Kirby was inside, I told Madeline and Carol about the basketball team that Kirby had played on the prior year. Several of our friends from Parkview had won the Missouri Boys' Club State Championship in St. Charles. Kirby had scored the winning basket by making an "old granny" free throw that hit the back of the rim, bounced three feet into the air, and came down through the hoop as time was running out. The team had gone on to represent Missouri in a regional tournament played in Terre Haute, Indiana.

A few minutes later, Kirby returned with a scruffy-looking kid, maybe nine or ten years old.

"This is Ernie," Kirby beamed. "He's learning to play basketball, and I've been helping him." Then Kirby proceeded to tell us about his volunteer work with underprivileged kids at the Boys' Club. I was totally unaware that he had been spending some of his free time with this program. Madeline and Carol were swept off their feet. Kirby had scored big points with the ladies.

After meeting Ernie and hearing what a noble "big brother" Kirby had been to him, the girls would have let us pick just about any movie we wanted to see. So we did. We chose "The Defiant Ones."

Tony Curtis and Sidney Poitier played the roles of prisoners who had escaped the law, hated one another, but were dependant upon each other to make their escape work. Theodore Bikel was the sheriff who stayed in hot pursuit. Not exactly your standard romantic date movie, but a classic nonetheless. Besides, the movie was just an excuse to have a date.

From there, we made the circuit through town: the city's square, Taylor's Drive-In, and then out to East Sunshine for a stop at Fisher's Hi-Boy. This was all about "seeing and being seen." Cars by the dozens drove through

Taylor's and Fisher's just to wave at friends and keep up with "who was dating whom."

"Oh, look!" Carol squealed. "There's Linda Hanks with Dick Davis. She and Dave Eustis have broken up."

Linda was the most popular girl in our class. She had been class homecoming attendant her freshman, sophomore, and junior years, and was a member of the Varsity Cheerleading Squad. She was every boy's dream but had been "off limits" for many months because of her going steady with Dave, a senior athlete.

"What's the deal with her and Dave?" Kirby inquired.

"Someone said Linda just wanted to be free to date other guys," Carol said.

"Lucky Davis," I said, only to catch a menacing glare from Carol.

Kirby took both of the girls home before heading for my house. On the way, he said, "I think I might ask Linda Hanks for a date."

Kirby
Parkview High School 1958-1959

PARKVIEW TASTEMARKS

*a*s the baseball season approached, there was great anticipation that the Parkview Vikings would make a mark for themselves in the Ozark Conference. Don Provance had become head baseball coach at the high school. Those of us who had played the year before were eager to show him what we could do on the ball field.

On more than one occasion, however, we conducted our practice sessions in Coach Provance's absence. He arranged for us to have access to the equipment room but then had other plans that prevented him from working with the team. Kirby and I were both in the starting lineup. We went winless in seven games, earning our athletic "letters" in disgrace.

"I don't give a rat's tail about the high school program," Kirby said after the brief season was over. "Things will be different this summer when we play Legion ball. Birmingham will whip us into shape."

Having a solid core of last year's starters returning, Dick Birmingham was excited about his prospects for the Parkview American Legion Junior baseball team in the summer of 1959. It was his third year to coach the Parkview Legion squad. He was unphased by the team's inability to win during the spring season under Coach Provance.

"That was then; this is now," Coach Birmingham kept telling us. "You guys are not a bunch of losers. All we need to do is get a few wins under our belt, and we can go all the way.

"Furthermore, I want you to picture yourselves in our new uniforms," Birmingham continued. "They are styled after the New York Yankees' pinstripes. The Yankees are winners, and this year we're going to be winners too."

Two days later, when Birmingham dismissed Dave Eustis, our best left-handed pitcher, for missing a couple of practices, some of us had our doubts. It was a wake-up call for sure, and the rest of us made certain we attended every practice or had an "iron-clad" excuse for not being there. Coach had made his point.

That year, Birmingham had scheduled thirty games to be played all over Southwest Missouri and into the three neighboring states. Our first "out-of-state" trip was to Tulsa, Oklahoma, where we stayed in the new downtown YMCA. Rain kept us from completing the games we had scheduled, and it was probably a good thing because none of us got much sleep. The gremlins—led by the playful Larry Westmoreland and his sidekick, Sam Mauck—were at work both nights.

"Where are you going?" Bill Lemery asked Westmoreland, his roommate.

"Out," replied the mischievous Westmoreland. "But cover for me if Birmingham comes by. Tell him I went downstairs to get some aspirin."

Several minutes later, Wes bolted into the room and fell into his bed. "Coach is coming," he gasped as he pulled the covers over his head and tried hard to assume a sleeping posture.

Seconds later, there was a rap at the door, and Coach Birmingham peered cautiously into the room.

"Lemery? Wes? Are you guys both here?" the weary coach inquired.

"Here, Coach," replied Bill.

"Yeah. What's up, Coach?" Wes moaned as if he had just been awakened.

"Get some sleep," Birmingham said as he shut the door.

No one may ever know what went down that night, but the rumors ran rampant. According to one team member, Sam Mauck had leaped from the top of our building to another building because he had seen a swimming pool on its roof. Someone else had stopped up the shower drains at the end of the hall and left the showers running all night. We awoke the next morning to two inches of water in the hallways. And our sponsor, Tastemark Dairy, received a bill to repair a busted door to one of our assigned rooms. We learned quickly that road trips could be a lot of fun.

Our next trip was over the Fourth of July weekend when we traveled to Bartlesville, Oklahoma, to play in a twelve-team tournament. We stayed in the barracks at a nearby air force base and limited our pranks to a few cherry bombs that were tossed in a timely manner into the mens bathroom. That just about put an end to our taking anymore overnight trips.

Jim Ratcliff, one of our hard-throwing right-handed pitchers, had grown up in a home with very limited financial resources. While in Bartlesville, all of us had our extra spending money except Jim. He had no cash and was too proud to take a handout from any of his teammates.

"We need to do something to help Jim get a little cash," Kirby whispered to Westmoreland and a few other members of the team. "Let's stage a poker game, and all of us lose a few bills so Jim can have some extra spending money." Jim had no clue, but at the end of a few rounds, he had enough cash to be on a par with the rest of us.

The next day, we had a pleasant surprise when we arrived at the Bartlesville City Stadium. A defunct minor league team had once used the baseball field for its home games. The stadium had dugouts, a grandstand, and a well-groomed grass infield. Our eyes were as big as saucers.

"This is what we need in Springfield," Phil Groover, our hard-hitting, slick-fielding third baseman kept saying as we took infield practice. "I could get used to a layout like this."

We won our first game against Claremore, Oklahoma, but were eliminated from the tournament in the second round by a superior team from Enid, Oklahoma. The score was 4–2.

After getting the season off to a 13–2 start and posting victories over teams from Missouri, Kansas, and Oklahoma, the Parkview Tastemarks hit the skids, losing seven of our next thirteen games. Parsons, Kansas, with a 20–2 record, defeated our star right-handed pitcher, Lynn Lambeth, 3–2, dropping his season record to 3–6. Things were beginning to look a bit grim.

On July 25, one week before district playoffs, we traveled to Jefferson City to play a team that had only lost one game in three years on its home field. The Central Missouri squad had beaten us earlier in the summer, 9–2, in Springfield. One of the few bright moments I had experienced all year was a two-run home run I hit in the bottom of the ninth to avert our being shut out.

Jeff City had a pitcher named Keith Weber who was unbeaten for the season. He threw harder than anyone we had faced all year. The game was not going to be easy, but Coach Birmingham convinced us it was exactly what we needed to get ready for the playoffs.

In the top half of the second inning, I dug into the batter's box for my first look at Weber. We were already behind 2–0, but the word on the bench was that we could get some runs off the right-hander if we would be patient and swing at good pitches. I was ready to do my part.

As Weber went into his windup, I cocked my bat and timed the movement of my stride to coincide with the speed of his pitch. In an instant, I saw the ball coming directly at my head and did what came naturally—I got out of the way. Everything except my right arm cleared the space. With a *crack* that could be heard throughout the grandstands, the ball smashed into my arm, just above the wrist. The pain was instant and severe. Tears welled up in my eyes as I picked myself up and walked slowly down to first base.

"Are you all right?" asked Coach Birmingham, who had trotted over from his third base coaching box.

"It's pretty sore," I said, trying not to say too much, lest he take me out of the game. "I'll be okay."

I could barely grip the ball during infield practice in the bottom half of the inning. Swinging a bat was even worse. This pain was not abating, and I was letting it show just a little too much.

"Are you going to be able to play or not?" demanded Kirby as we sat next to each other in the dugout. "I know you're hurt, but don't stay in the lineup at the expense of the team. We have a ballgame to win tonight, and you're not helping us by walking around the dugout, grimacing in pain."

He was right, of course. I was thinking mostly about myself, while Kirby was looking after the welfare of our team. I remained in the game, however, contributing nothing at the plate and struggling in the field. Although we out hit Jeff City 7–4, we lost the game, 5–4. Weber had escaped with another victory.

The next morning, Dad drove me to the hospital in Springfield to have X-rays taken of my arm.

"He has broken his right ulna just above the wrist," the radiologist explained to my dad. "Fortunately, it's cracked, but still in place. We won't have to set the arm, but it will need to be in a cast for five to six weeks."

That wasn't the news I wanted to hear. The playoffs were about to begin, and my season was over. The doctor proceeded to wrap my aching arm in a plaster cast that extended from the hand up to within an inch of my right elbow. Using my left hand, I placed a telephone call to Coach Birmingham and broke the news.

CRUNCH TIME

*A*lthough the Parkview Tastemarks brought a 20–10 record into the playoffs, we were not given a huge chance to unseat our crosstown rivals, Central Pepsi. They were defending district champions, state runner-up finishers last season, and had beaten us all three times we had met during the current year. The tournament was a five-team, double-elimination event and, by the luck of the draw, we were pitted against Central in the first game.

"Listen up," came those familiar words from Coach Birmingham. "The playoffs are like a whole new season. You're a better team than Central. Now go out there and show this crowd what you're made of."

At the end of five innings, we were leading Central 2–0. Lynn Lambeth was tough on the mound and had been supported with some timely hits from Dick Davis, Phil Groover, Sam Mauck, and John Hammon. But

Central scored eight runs in the last four innings to take an 8–3 victory, sending us into the losers' bracket. We would have to win five consecutive games in order to become district champions.

Our second game was a laugher, taking us only six innings to wrap up a 17–0 victory over Ava. Kirby had two hits in the eleven-run fifth inning that put the game on ice. Branson Brown pitched the no-hit shut out. Good pitching from Jim Ratcliff and Jerry Edwards produced victories over Hillcrest and West Plains in games three and four, leaving only two teams left in the tournament— Parkview Tastemarks and our nemesis, Central Pepsi.

Central was undefeated in the playoffs, which meant we would have to win twice in order to advance. No one had to tell us that we had lost four straight games to them. On top of that, Central had a fifteen-game winning streak on the line.

To make matters worse, three of our starters were sidelined with injuries. Dick Davis was out with a concussion he had suffered the previous evening; Sam Mauck had been hit by a pitch, breaking his cheekbone; and I was out with my broken arm. And, coming through the losers' bracket, our pitching staff had been stretched thin. Odds of our winning the district playoffs were not that good.

Earlier in the year, Birmingham had named Kirby

and me co-captains of our team. As we prepared to take the field against Central, Kirby rose to the occasion and asked if he could say a few words.

"Look," Kirby began, "I hate losing to these guys. We've worked too hard this year to let it get away from us now. Let's go out there and play like the champions we know we are." It was good leadership on his part. The team needed a hard poke in the ribs, or wherever it would help the most.

The first six innings developed into a pitchers' duel between Central's unbeaten ace, Larry Taunt, and our best hurler, Lynn Lambeth. Both teams had been unable to score, and base runners were scarce. The tension on the field and in the stands had become palpable.

In the top of the seventh, Central scored the game's first run with two singles and a successful squeeze play. They carried that 1–0 lead into the bottom of the ninth. It had come down to this: We would have to score at least one run or hang up our spikes for the season.

Lambeth led off our half of the ninth, working Taunt to a 3–1 count. Birmingham was getting desperate for some base runners, so he flashed Lynn the "take" sign. The next pitch was a fastball that caught too much of the plate.

Whether Lynn missed the sign or ignored it, no one can be sure, but with one powerful swing of the bat, he smashed the ball over the center field chain-linked fence, clearing it by at least fifteen feet. It was the best result from a "take" sign that we had seen all year. That blast ignited the fire in our hearts and in our quiet bats.

Following the home run, Bill Lemery was hit by a pitch, advancing to third on a single by Kirby. Phil Groover hammered one of Taunt's servings down the third-base line to drive in the winning run in a sweet 2–1, come-from-behind victory. The Central hex had been broken.

Winning the second game against Central was equally important. The loser was finished for the year. Kirby led a hit parade with four of our sixteen hits, while driving in three runs, as we took the nightcap, 11–8, advancing to the Missouri Western Zone Playoffs for the first time. The next day's newspaper ran a large article on the game, including our team picture, and carried the photo caption "District Champs." That was good, of course, but there was more work ahead of us.

In order to compete in the Missouri State Championship game, a team had to survive its district playoffs and then defeat the three other top teams in the Western or Eastern Zone. Joplin, Carrollton, and North Kansas City were all as eager as we were to advance from the Western Zone and play in the championship game in

Jefferson City. Once again, the tournament was double elimination.

Lynn Lambeth was tapped by Birmingham to be our starting pitcher in the first game of the Western Zone playoffs. He responded by striking out the first nine North Kansas City batters he faced and went on to strike out fourteen, pitching a one-hit shutout, 2–0. The lone hit, a single, came with two outs in the ninth. My replacement at second base, Branson Brown, was our hitting star, scoring one run and driving in the other. That victory put us into the winners' bracket for the first time in the playoffs. Our next foe was Joplin, a team we had beaten twice during the regular season.

Jerry Edwards and Jim Ratcliff combined for a three-hitter, enabling us to whip Joplin 12–2. When Joplin went on to defeat North Kansas City in the losers' bracket finals, we recognized they were in the same position we had been in during the district playoffs with Central. Joplin had not beaten us all year, and they would have to win two in order to advance.

Joplin got off to a quick start, plating three runs in the first three innings. We came back to tie the game in the fifth, and that was all the scoring from either team until the ninth. Back-to-back singles by Donnie Haworth, Bill Lemery, Kirby, and Dick Davis brought in two runs and a chance to win the game in regulation.

But Joplin scored two runs in the bottom of the ninth, sending us into extra innings.

After three scoreless frames, we erupted for seven runs in the top of the thirteenth inning. It should have been enough to punch our ticket to the Missouri State Championship game. However, Joplin, playing its second extra-inning game in a row, was not finished. With two men out, they scored five runs in the bottom of the thirteenth before Coach called on Lambeth to come off the bench and get the final out.

Parkview Tastemarks were Western Zone Champions. Next stop, Jefferson City!

MR. CLUTCH

*D*ick Birmingham had calculated that the Parkview Tastemarks had traveled 3,192 miles during the summer of 1959 and had played twenty-one road games in four different states. He wasn't afraid of facing Jefferson City on their home field, Washington Park, even though they had only lost one game at home in the last three years.

"That was then, this is now," he reminded us with one of his favorite rallying cries.

A Springfield newspaper reporter had corralled Birmingham before we left for Jefferson City and asked him about our chances against a team that had beaten us twice during the year and had one of the state's most formidable pitchers, Keith Weber, ready to face us in the first game.

"We have as good a club as they have," Birmingham told the reporter. "We have a better all-around club, but they've got stronger pitching." He went on to clarify,

"On a given day, any of our pitchers can be as strong as any of them, and Lambeth can be a little tougher."

Our sponsors were more than happy to charter a bus for us to make the journey to Jefferson City. Hotel accommodations were arranged at the renowned Missouri Hotel. This was the trip we had been dreaming about ever since the season began. As we unloaded our luggage and baseball gear in front of the hotel, we couldn't help but wonder if this was what it was like to travel with a minor league professional team.

"This is cool, man," Ricky Davis said in the vernacular of the day.

"Do we get room service?" Sam Mauck asked for all to hear.

We were all caught up in the moment and enjoying a celebratory mood. Before the afternoon was over, we would have to concentrate on the mission that had brought us to the state's capital city.

Jefferson City had won the Eastern Zone playoffs, defeating a talented St. Louis Aubochon Dennison squad. We were mindful that they were playing with a "home field" advantage at Washington Park. A flip of the coin, however, gave us the "home team" designation for the first game. When the umpire yelled, "Play ball!" Lynn Lambeth was on the mound, ready to throw the first pitch.

For seven scoreless innings, Lynn matched Keith

Weber pitch for pitch. In the bottom of the sixth, we had threatened to break the 0–0 tie when Donnie Haworth led off the inning with a single. Bill Lemery grounded into a fielder's choice, forcing Donnie at second base. Kirby followed with a double, but Bill was held at third. Weber bore down at that point, and the next two batters hit weak ground balls back to the pitcher.

In the top of the eighth, Jefferson City drew first blood. Keith Weber, a triple threat on any athletic field, hit his own three-bagger and later scored on a wild pitch. Now we needed to play "catch-up" ball against this hard-throwing phenom who had shown us no mercy. We did not get it done in the bottom of the eighth and, once again, found ourselves down 1–0 as we approached the bottom of the ninth.

Whenever we needed to score runs, it was our good fortune if our third baseman, Phil Groover, was scheduled to hit in that frame. One newspaper reporter had described Phil as a "gritty little player," and that seemed to fit the way he played the game. He was a "hard out."

"Come on, Phil, you gritty little player, you!" John Hammon, our right-fielder, yelled as Phil approached the plate. "Show us something!"

And Phil did. With one crack of the bat, he unloaded on Weber with a triple of his own and was chased home one out later on a single by Sam Mauck. We had dodged the bullet and forced the game into extra innings.

By Legion rules, no pitcher could pitch more than twelve innings in a twenty-four-hour period. When Lynn Lambeth came to bat in the bottom of the twelfth with the game still tied 1–1, he was finished with his pitching chores for the evening. The bullpen would have to hold Jefferson City in the thirteenth inning if the game was not won in the bottom of the twelfth. Weber was also finishing his last frame as we came to bat.

Lynn reached first base on an error to start the bottom half of the twelfth inning. I was coaching at first base and called to the dugout for someone to bring Lynn a jacket. Then I heard Birmingham call time.

After conferring with the Jefferson City coach and the Legion commissioner, Birmingham began walking toward first base.

He pointed at me and said, "I want you to run for Lambeth."

Still wearing a plaster cast on my right arm, I had no clue that Coach Birmingham would ask me to play in this critical game. Because the cast extended from my hand to a point just below the elbow, it didn't inhibit my movement in any way. A strip of plaster stretching across my right palm did prevent me from gripping a bat or a ball. Being asked to pinch run, however, was no problem.

Donnie Haworth, our shortstop and leadoff hitter, was at the plate. While taking a cautious lead off first base, I saw Birmingham give Donnie the "bunt" sign. Coach was playing percentage baseball by trying to get a runner in scoring position.

Donnie laid down a perfect bunt, forcing the third baseman to field the ball and make the throw to first. I was on my way to second the moment the bat touched the ball.

As I approached second base, taking a peek at the bunt to see whether it might be necessary for me to slide, I saw the play unfolding and knew there was no play to be made at second. What I also saw was that third base was left totally unattended because the shortstop was covering second and the third baseman was practically all the way to home plate. Without breaking stride, I rounded second base and headed for third. In my mind, there was no doubt I could make it.

The play at third was much closer than I had thought it would be. I went into the bag with my best feet-first slide and my cast held high in the air. When the dust cleared, the umpire yelled, "Safe!" Birmingham, who would have broken my other arm if the umpire had called me out, began to breathe once again. We had a runner on third with only one out.

One out later, Kirby "Clutch" Wilcox stepped up to the plate. Birmingham went though his series of signs, but we all knew Kirby was cleared to "hit away." He had a confident look in his eye as he assumed his stance, glaring over his left shoulder toward the hard-throwing right-hander.

Our entire team would have settled for anything to score the run at this point—an error, a wild pitch, a balk—anything! Kirby wanted his fourth hit of the night, and that is exactly what he got—a clean single into left center field to drive in the winning run. We had beaten the invincible Keith Weber 2–1 and claimed the first win in the best-of-three-game series.

Rain postponed the second game until Monday. It was a woolly affair with Jefferson City taking a 7–4 lead after two innings. But Jerry Edwards came in to pitch in relief and held our opponents scoreless the last seven innings. Once again, Kirby led a ten-hit attack that resulted in a 9–7 Parkview victory and clinched the state championship two games to none.

Winning a state championship in almost any type of competitive event is a defining moment in the lives of the participants. It becomes part of their identity for years to come. What the Parkview Tastemarks lacked in raw talent we made up for in "heart." Time and again, we came back to snatch victory from the jaws of defeat. It was an incredible group of guys led by a remarkable coach.

The season ended in McPherson, Kansas, where we were successful in defeating the Kansas and Iowa state champions, but lost the regional tournament to an excellent team from Enid, Oklahoma.

SENIOR SWAGGER

*a*s our senior year began at Parkview, students had new respect for members of the baseball team. No longer were we the "winless wonders" of the Ozark Conference, as was the case during the past spring. Now, wearing our new Parkview Tastemark Legion jackets with the state tournament patches sewn on the front, we walked the halls of Parkview High with a swagger befitting champions.

Those early morning student gatherings in the school's lobby, prior to the start of our first-hour classes, allowed us the opportunity to regale our friends with highlights from our summer triumphs. But, as we soon discovered, it was September, and the sport of current interest was Viking football.

"You guys need to buy a ribbon to show your support for the football team," said Linda Hanks as she approached Kirby and me one morning. "The first game is this Friday against Springdale."

Linda, dressed in her green cheerleader sweater and gold skirt, flashed a coy smile that would have knocked any teenage boy off his feet. Kirby was prepared for the moment.

"If I agree to buy one of your ribbons, will you let me ask you out for a date after the game?" Kirby teased.

"Maybe," Linda replied. "Why don't you pay twice the price for your ribbon and take your chances?" I sensed some chemistry working between the two of them but wasn't sure where it would lead.

Kirby was on the varsity football team and was taking some tough senior courses. He and I both maintained good grades, taking our studies seriously. While football consumed many of his after-school hours, I spent most of my spare time working with student government.

Just prior to the close of our junior year, I had been elected student body president for the coming fall. My opponents were very popular athletes—Larry Westmoreland, captain of the football team, and Bob Payne, captain of the basketball team. With the two of them splitting votes from one major sector of the student electorate, I eked by with the victory.

"You are one lucky son of a gun," Kirby had said to me after the election results were announced. "Almost everyone I know voted for Wes or Payne. How on earth did you pull that off?"

"Beats me," I replied. "I wonder about that myself."

Each year since its opening, Parkview had exchanged "student talent assemblies" with Central High School. That fall we would also be exchanging talent shows with the new school on the north side of town, Hillcrest High. One of my assignments as student body president was to extend a greeting from Parkview to the students at the other schools.

John Ashcroft was the newly elected student body president of Hillcrest. He was also the quarterback for their football team. Dick Birmingham, who had begun teaching at Hillcrest, was his backfield coach. I called John to check on some details for our upcoming visit to his school.

"John, how's the year going?" I asked.

"Great, except for some tough times on the gridiron," he replied. "You guys showed us no mercy."

We chatted about a few other matters and then he surprised me.

"How's Kirby Wilcox doing?" John asked. "He and I went to school together at Hickory Hills, and we played on a Kiwanis League baseball team that his dad coached."

"Kirby's having a great year," I replied. "He lettered

on the football team that won the Ozark Conference title, and he's dating Linda Hanks, our homecoming queen. I don't think he could be doing much better."

The year rolled along with the perfect mix of academic challenges, athletic achievements, and social engagements. We took our college placement exams and began to apply for the universities that were of interest to us. I made a visit to the University of Missouri in Columbia with a classmate, Kurt Watkins, but knew all along that my heart was set on attending Southern Methodist University in Dallas.

Kirby also made the trek to Columbia. On a rainy day in March, he took Bill Lemery, Don Riesenberg, and Tommy Thompson in his Ford convertible to see what "Mizzou" was all about. Meanwhile, he had his eyes set on higher stakes. Kirby definitely wanted to take a crack at an appointment to West Point. The University of Missouri might have been a good alternative, but it was not his first choice

The Parkview baseball season was more successful than the 0–7 record we had attained the year before, but it ended in ironic disappointment. Our hearts were set on competing for the state title, as we had done in the Legion program, only this time the decisive game would be played in Busch Stadium in St. Louis, home of our beloved Cardinals. As it turned out, Hillcrest High, the new kids on the block, coached by our former Legion coach, Dick Birmingham, knocked us out of the play-offs, ending our season sooner than we had anticipated.

One day in the lunchroom, I encountered Don Riesenberg, one of Kirby's more cerebral friends, who happened to be a lifelong chum of mine.

"Have you heard about Wilcox?" Don asked.

"No. What's up?" I said

"He's in St. John's Hospital," Don said with a worried expression on his face. "They have him quarantined. I think he has a staph infection."

That evening, I drove to the hospital, slipped past the nurses, and surprised Kirby with my visit.

"What's the deal?" I said. "You aren't getting enough attention at school, so you have to pull a stunt like this?"

"It's nothing." He laughed. "I've just got a boil on my foot. Doesn't seem that bad to me, but the doctors and my mom are all in a tizzy over it.

"Listen, I need for you to do me a favor," Kirby continued. "I'm not going to be able to take Linda to the prom next weekend. Can you stand in for me?"

"What I hear you saying is that you need someone who poses absolutely no threat of stealing your girlfriend away from you to take her to the prom," I responded. "Is that it?"

"Something like that," he said and chuckled.

That was the only date I ever had with Linda Hanks. When I called for her at her house and presented her with a corsage for the evening, she was as beautiful as a cover girl on a fashion magazine. We danced until the party was over, chatting mostly about Kirby and why we both thought he was a pretty special guy.

Early word of Kirby's appointment to West Point came just before our high school graduation in May. He was to report that summer to the prestigious Academy on the west bank of the Hudson River in faraway New York. Although he and Linda had deep feelings for one another, they had agreed that time and space required that they not place fetters on themselves.

Linda had chosen to attend William Jewell College in Liberty, Missouri. It was "light years" away from Kirby's new world in New York. Being realistic about their respective futures, they decided it would be best if they were able to date and build new relationships. Although always intending to be dear friends, they were free to go their separate ways.

DRIFTING APART

*B*ecause my birthday happened to fall in October, I was eligible for one more season of American Legion Junior baseball. Kirby was not. Even if he were eligible, his orders to report to West Point would have precluded him from playing that summer.

Dick Birmingham was now coaching the Hillcrest Legion team, leaving Parkview open for a new coach. Of all people, Kirby's dad, Charlie Wilcox, volunteered to take a crack at the vacated position. Looking back, I would have to say he did a fine job.

The team did not have many of the key players who had led Parkview to the state championship in 1959, but Lynn Lambeth still had a year of eligibility, and that alone made the team a contender. Kirby came out to a few of our practices, hitting fungoes to the outfielders and shooting the breeze with some of us who had played with him the year before.

"You guys don't look like a ball club," Kirby chided as he played catch with a few of us in the outfield.

"You have no hustle, no determination in your eyes," he continued. "Birmingham's going to whip your backsides if you don't tighten things up."

The Parkview Tastemarks took a few road trips, played some good baseball, and beat Birmingham's young Hillcrest squad in the playoffs to repeat as district champions.

The Western Zone Playoffs were held in Clinton, Missouri, about halfway between Springfield and Kansas City. I had three of the best games of my Legion career, knocking the cover off the baseball and making some circus catches in center field. Early in the season, Mr. Wilcox had moved me from second base to Kirby's old position in center field.

"I'm making this move for defensive purposes," was Mr. Wilcox's diplomatic way of saying, "You're making too many errors in the infield."

The Parkview Tastemarks breezed through that double-elimination tournament and were certified to play, once again, for the state championship in Jefferson City. If we could have managed two more victories, we would have secured another state title for Springfield. Our opponent that year was a heavy-hitting team from St. Louis.

The Eastern Zone champs won both title games, leaving Parkview Legion Post 69 as the 1960 state runner-up.

On June 4, Kirby's eighteenth birthday, he received a telegram with the "official announcement" that he was accepted into West Point. It was a heady experience and one that carried with it some active-duty military commitments once he graduated from the Academy. To accept the position also meant he would likely not be able to pursue a career in professional baseball.

"Dad, I'm not sure what I should do," he confided to Mr. Wilcox that evening. "What do you think?"

"Kirby," his dad began, "this needs to be your decision. Your mom and I do not plan to sway you in either direction. It's a big decision and one you need to make, because you're the one who will live with the consequences."

What made his choice especially difficult was a proposal from a professional baseball scout, Tom Greenwade, who had signed Mickey Mantle to a contract with the New York Yankees a decade earlier. Now Mr. Greenwade was prepared to offer Kirby a baseball scholarship to the University of Southern California. He could have gotten his education and been given a crack at a career in professional baseball, one of his lifelong dreams. After some deep soul searching, however, Kirby chose to attend West Point.

Kirby and I said our "good-byes" one afternoon, knowing that our friendship would be tested by distance and new theaters of influence in our lives. He promised to write, as did I. He left for New York, and a few weeks later, I packed up my footlocker and headed for Dallas. From that time forward, Springfield was mostly about our past. His future and mine lay elsewhere.

Kirby and I were both home a few days for Christmas. He shared with me what it was like to be a plebe at a military academy.

"You can't imagine how tough the upperclassmen can be on first-year students," Kirby began. "As a plebe, I have no time of my own, and the hazing is brutal."

"The Phi Delt 'rallies' are no picnic for us Phikeias either," I tried to counter.

He could only laugh at how little I comprehended what he was going through at West Point.

The next spring Charlie and Bettye Wilcox made the trip to West Point to visit their son and attend parade exercises on the Commons. They took Kirby's sister, Patti, and one of her high school friends. There were 1,182 uniformed plebes marching on the field that afternoon.

"That's Kirby over there in the third unit to your left," Mr. Wilcox said to his wife as they watched the proceedings. "He's the second one back on the left outside row."

"Charles, how can you possibly know that?" replied Mrs. Wilcox. "There are hundreds of boys out there and they are all dressed alike."

"Because I know my son's gait," Mr. Wilcox responded with a wink and a smile. "That's the way Kirby walks. I would know it anywhere."

After the ceremonies were over, Kirby had some private time with his family.

"Son, tell your mother which unit you were in," Mr. Wilcox pressed the issue, "and tell her which position you were in among the group."

Kirby confirmed what his dad had already surmised. He was in the third unit, second row, left outside column. Uniforms can't hide everything about a person.

When baseball season came around, Kirby and I both answered the bell. He played for the freshman squad at Army; I lettered for the freshmen Ponies at SMU. We shared a note or two about our successes, knowing that none of what we did in college ball could compare to that championship season we had experienced together in the summer of 1959.

Kirby and I graduated from college in 1964—he from West Point, and I from Oklahoma Christian College in Oklahoma City. Three weeks before graduation, I married my college sweetheart, Martha Mitchell, and received my acceptance letter to attend Southern Methodist University Law School that fall. Kirby was making plans for four years of active military duty.

Our paths crossed again in Springfield that summer, three months before I began law school in Dallas. I was working a sales route for Swift and Company and preaching on Sundays for a small church in Shell Knob. Martha was employed at Heer's Department Store in the credit department.

"Guess who I met today at work," Martha said when she arrived home one evening.

"I give up. Who?" I said, not wanting to play "twenty questions."

"Linda Hanks. Kirby's girlfriend," she answered. "She works at Heer's. I think they're dating again."

What I hadn't known was that for much of their senior year, Kirby and Linda had been corresponding with one another. Their warm relationship had begun to sizzle once more. Kirby returned to Springfield with full expectation of seeing Linda, and she too anticipated renewing the courtship.

Two months later, Martha and I attended their wedding, wishing them joy, eternal love, and years of happiness together. It was the perfect ending for their fairy-tale romance. The handsome prince, clad in his military dress uniform, had come home to wed his lovely princess. Now they were one in heart and soul, ready to live happily ever after.

Kirby
West Point 1965

FOR HIS FRIENDS

*O*ne dreadfully hot day in August 1964, Martha and I loaded up our un-air-conditioned Dodge Dart and headed for our new life in Dallas, Texas. The car was packed to its ceiling, with the ironing board wedged in at the very top. If the casting director for *The Beverly Hillbillies* had seen us, he would have signed us up on the spot.

Martha accepted a job in the publications office of Texas Instruments, while I took a full load of classes at SMU's law school and worked part-time as a youth minister for a local church. Before either of us received a paycheck, we were down to eighty-seven cents in our pockets, and Martha needed to buy a can of Aqua Net Hair Spray. Fortunately, it only cost seventy-nine cents. We weren't broke yet.

That October the St. Louis Cardinals were playing the New York Yankees in the World Series. Being from

Missouri, I was an avid St. Louis fan and wore my Cardinal cap daily in support of the team. It had been eighteen long years since the Redbirds had made it to the Series.

At one of our church youth outings, I noticed that M.L. Aday, Jr., a senior at Thomas Jefferson High School, was wearing a Yankee cap. M.L. played for his high school baseball team and also sang with a student rock band. I wanted to get to know him better, so I approached him about the Series.

"What makes you a Yankee fan?" I asked to break the ice.

"Just like 'em," he replied.

"Do you think you might want to play professional baseball someday?" I asked, knowing that playing Major League ball was almost every high school player's dream.

"I guess so, if I'm good enough," he said. "But there are some other things I would like to do as well."

We visited at length about the Series. I told him about our Parkview Legion team that had won the state championship and about my friend Kirby who had just finished West Point. There were some things about M.L. that reminded me of Kirby. He said he wanted to play baseball in college next fall, and I offered to help him get a scholarship.

Meanwhile, Kirby and Linda were caught up in a series of sad farewells and joyful reunions. Two weeks after their wedding, Kirby shipped out to Ft. Benning, Georgia, where he reported for Paratrooper School. Linda moved back to North Kansas City to fulfill a teaching contract. It wasn't the way they wanted to spend their first year of marriage, but both felt obliged to keep their respective commitments.

While Linda was still in Kansas City, Kirby was given a one-month leave before being assigned to active duty in Korea.

"I only have a month," Kirby said one night on the phone. "Can you find a place for us to spend that time together before I deploy to Korea?"

Linda had been living in some apartments with a couple of college friends. She secured a studio apartment in the same complex, and there she and Kirby spent four whole weeks together. It was the longest stretch of wedded bliss the two would have for another year. Kirby spent the next twelve months in South Korea, serving as a general's aide.

Upon returning to the States, Kirby was stationed for three months at Ft. Knox, Kentucky. Linda was able to be with him. Their next assignment took both of them overseas—this time to Germany, a popular staging area for military units destined for Vietnam. While in Germany, Kirby would be in the field for weeks at a time— gone three weeks, home one.

The war in Vietnam had begun to heat up. An alarming number of troops from the United States were being sent into the conflict. American television networks carried live reports from the battlefields. For most viewers, Southeast Asia was so remote that they had no comprehension of why it was necessary for United States Military Forces to be engaged in what appeared to be localized civil strife.

Kirby was in Germany one year before he volunteered for assignment in Vietnam. He was not one to shirk his obligations. This is what he had prepared himself to do. It was time for him to step up to the line. In August 1967, two months after the birth of his son, Curt, Kirby was deployed to Vietnam as Captain Charles K. Wilcox.

Back in the less-stressful surroundings of Dallas, Texas, I had a student deferment that kept me from the military draft while in law school. But the rules on those deferments were always subject to change.

One day I returned to our apartment, having just finished a final exam in International Law. In the mailbox I found an envelope that I had been dreading to receive. It was from the Selective Service office in Springfield.

"What does it mean?" Martha asked as we reread every sentence word by word.

"It means that I have to report for a physical," I said soberly. "It's the first step before being drafted."

I kept the appointment, took my physical, but was never called for military service. Whether it was a high draft number, or my work in ministry, or the birth of our first child that kept me out of the armed forces, I never knew for sure. It was an unsettling time in my life, and one I have replayed in my mind many times since.

I will never forget the call I received from my parents in January 1968. They were both on the line, and my dad, who was usually jovial, spoke in a solemn tone.

"We just received word that Kirby has been killed in Vietnam," Dad said.

He paused. I paused. The whole world paused while I tried to make sense of his words.

"Say again, Dad," I managed to say with a lump in my throat.

"The time of the funeral service has not been set, but we will let you know as soon as we hear something," Dad went on to say. I could hear my mother crying in the background.

I hung up the phone and bawled like a baby.

The emotions that came over me the next few days are still difficult to describe. I felt shame and guilt for not being in a foxhole next to my friend. I felt anger that Americans were being asked to pay the ultimate sacrifice in a country so remote from my everyday world. Most of all, I felt a huge void in my heart for the loss of a friend.

The funeral was held in Springfield, and Kirby's body was interred at the National Cemetery on the south side of town. The white marker over his grave is like so many others that remind us of those who have given their lives in defense of the freedoms we enjoy as a nation. Kirby, and all who have bravely worn the uniform in battle, must not be forgotten.

> "Greater love has no one than this: that he lay down his life for his friends."
>
> John 15:13, NIV

EPILOGUE

STEVE ROGERS, the ten-year-old pitcher for the Mustangs, played college baseball while attending the University of Tulsa. A few years later, he became a Major League Baseball star for the Montreal Expos. He was an All-Star for five seasons and was the National League's starting pitcher in the 1982 All-Star game in Montreal.

JOHN ASHCROFT, the student body president at Hillcrest High School, became governor of Missouri, a United States senator from Missouri, and the attorney general of the United States during the first term of President George W. Bush. He currently heads the Ashcroft Group, a lobbying organization in Washington, D.C.

CHARLES MCCORD, the piano player in the Four Flames and Two Flickers, teamed up with Don Imus of "Imus in the Morning," reporting the news on national radio and television each weekday.

M.L. ADAY, JR., the high school baseball player in my Dallas church youth group, became an internationally acclaimed rock star, using the moniker "Meatloaf."

DICK BIRMINGHAM coached high school and Legion baseball for more than twenty-five years in Springfield, before retiring to run a sports camp. He and his wife, Rosemary, have four children. Dick was named to the Missouri's Sports Hall of Fame and has received other prestigious awards for his years of coaching.

CHARLES and **BETTYE WILCOX** still reside in the home on East Sunset where Kirby grew up as a boy. It is only two blocks from the National Cemetery where Kirby was buried. Their daughter, Patti Dusel, resides in California.

LINDA HANKS WILCOX LINDSAY gave birth to a son seven months before Kirby's death. His name is Curt. Linda married Keith H. Lindsay in 1969, and they resided in Lake Wales, Florida, for many years prior to his death in 2007. She also keeps a home in Ozark, Missouri.

Parkview Tastemarks

Back Row: Dick Birmingham (coach), Jerry Edwards, J.D. Hall, Bill Lemery, Larry Westmoreland, Jim Ratcliff, Lynn Lambeth, Sam Mauck, and Branson Brown.

Front Row: Bobby Dobbs, Dick Davis, John Hammon, Kirby Wilcox, Terry Johnson, Rick Davis, Donnie Haworth, and Phil Groover.